Youth Volleyball
Championship Skills

Terry Liskevych & Don Patterson

MASTERS PRESS

A Division of Howard W. Sams & Company

Published by Masters Press
(A Division of Howard W. Sams & Co.)
2647 Waterfront Pkwy. E. Drive, Suite 100
Indianapolis, IN 46214

   98 99 00 01 02   10 9 8 7 6 5 4

Library of Congress Cataloging-in-Publication Data

Liskevych, Terry, 1948-
    Youth volleyball: championship skills / Terry Liskevych &
Don Patterson.
        p.   cm.
    ISBN 1-57028-028-2 (pbk.)
    1. Volleyball for children. I. Patterson, Don, 1963-. II. Title.
GV1015.4.C55L57   1995   95-16789
796.325'083--dc20   CIP

Table of Contents

Acknowledgments

I would like to thank all the players I have coached in the last 25 years. A special thanks to 1992 Olympic bronze medalists Tara Cross-Battle, Lori Endicott, Tammy Liley, Elaina Oden, Teee Williams and Yoko Zetterlund, who demonstrated the skills for this book's photo shoot.

Also, thanks to Greg Giovanazzi, the women's coach at the University of Michigan, and USA Assistant Coach Kent Miller for their review of the manuscript.

And finally, to Wilson Sporting Goods Company for their support.

Credits:
Photos by Robert Beck and Mitchell Layton
Cover design by Kelli Ternet
Diagrams by Phil Velikan
Edited by Heather Seal

INTRODUCTION

When I decided I wanted to be a coach, the first thing I did was read and reread every book on volleyball that I could find. There weren't many. It was the early '70s, and volleyball was nowhere near as popular then as it is today.

It gave me a good start, though. And with that base of knowledge, I continued to learn about the game, sometimes through conversations with other coaches, other times just by trying new techniques to see if they worked.

My purpose in writing this book is to take the knowledge I have acquired over the years and pass it along to you in simple, visual descriptions. If you can master all the skills in this book, you'll be a valuable member of your team.

But keep in mind, the improvement won't just automatically happen once you've read the book. To become a great player, you need to take this information and use it. And the way you do that is by playing as much as possible.

Most of all, remember this: Volleyball is a great game. So enjoy it and have fun.

Terry Liskevych

USA Volleyball

Caren Kemner — 1988 and 1992 Olympian

CUE WORDS AND KEY PHRASES

You'll notice that throughout this book there are cue words and key phrases at the beginning of each chapter. I've done this to help you remember the important points of the different skills so you can concentrate on them during matches.

To start off with, let's cover two cue words and key phrases that every volleyball player should apply at all times, whether they are practicing or playing a match.

Cue word: *Anticipate*
Key phrase: — Never be surprised
— Expect every ball to come to you

Cue word: *Focus*
Key phrase: — Keep eyes on the ball
— Maintain focus for entire play, rally, practice, game, match

A review of all cue words and key phrases can be found on pages 115-117.

Oleg Shatunov —Russian player

I. Movement

Cue word: *Feet*
Key phrase: — Beat ball to spot
                           — Stay on feet as much as possible

Cue word: — *Ready*
Key phrase: — Balanced to move in any direction

When you watch great players like Karch Kiraly and Caren Kemner, one thing that really stands out is the way they make almost every play look routine. The average volleyball fan is easily fooled into thinking that the best player on the court is the one who is always making spectacular dives. But when a player is always diving and sprawling, it's usually because he or she is out of position.

You should wear knee pads for protection in case you have to hit the floor in an emergency situation, not so you can do bellyflops on the hardwood.

Great players will read the play, make a quick, smooth adjustment and intersect the ball. Next time you're watching a high-level volleyball match, train your eyes on the best passer rather than watching the path of the serve.

By the time most fans have shifted their eyes to catch up with the action, a great player won't even be moving. Again, the key is reading and moving efficiently. It may not be spectacular, but it makes coaches happy.

Moving quickly and getting into a balanced, stationary position before the ball arrives is important. Your goal as the passer/digger is to form a stable base so you get a clean rebound off your arms. Volleyball is a lot different from many other popular American sports. In baseball, football and basketball, one of your main objectives is to catch the ball. And you can do that just as well running as you can standing. But since volleyball is a rebound sport, one split-second contact determines the difference between a good play and a bad play. That's where movement without the ball becomes important. If you can react and move to the right spot so you're in a balanced, stationary position when you contact the ball, you'll make a good dig or pass. If you can't, all you do is build up the setter's endurance for distance running by sending him all over the court to track down your unpredictable passes, digs, etc.

Your area

For starters, let's talk about your responsibilities. A lot of players try to cover too much territory and do more harm than good. When you are in the back court, your range will never be greater than four feet in any direction. Coaches sometimes train kids by throwing a ball out of their reach and saying, "Go dive for it." That's pointless. You should practice digging or passing balls that are realistically within your range. Anything beyond four feet should be handled by a player who's closer to the ball. Don't make a lot of needless dives, rolls or sprawls.

Ready position

While you're reading the action on the other side, you need to be in a position that enables you to move your whole body quickly, in any direction. We'll call this medium posture. Here are the keys:

1. **Feet** shoulder-width apart.

2. One foot slightly in front of the other.

3. Heels off the floor, weight distributed on the balls and insides of the feet.

4. Knees bent slightly.

5. Shoulders in front of the knees.

6. Knees in front of the feet.

7. Back bent slightly forward.

8. Hands and arms above the knees and away from the body.

Lori Endicott demonstrates the ready position — front and side views

Moving side to side

Once you're comfortable with the medium posture you can begin learning lateral movement. I've found that the best way to move a short distance is to step-hop quickly, side to side. If you have to move farther, you might take two or three steps, but the important thing is to end the motion with a hop.

When you hop, lift both **feet** off the ground at the same time but keep them close to the floor. They should be shoulder width apart. Don't take cross-over steps. That's an easy way to lose your balance, and it makes it difficult to face the target area. The step-hop ensures stability.

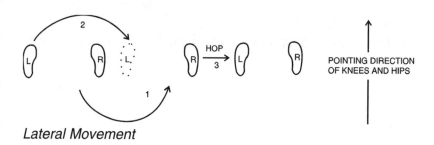

Lateral Movement

1. 2. 3.

4. 5.

Teee Williams demonstrates step-hopping to her left

Moving up and back

To move forward, face the direction you want to go and use normal running steps. Your knees and hips should be pointed in the direction you're moving. Before you make contact with the ball, pivot your knees and hips and point to the target area. Forward movement is most common for three skills: serve reception, spiking approach and the first step of a defensive or emergency situation. In serve reception, you can either hop forward or move forward with a step followed by a hop. Using a step-hop side to side motion and a step-hop motion up and back, three, four or five players can easily cover the court if they are in a W serve reception pattern.

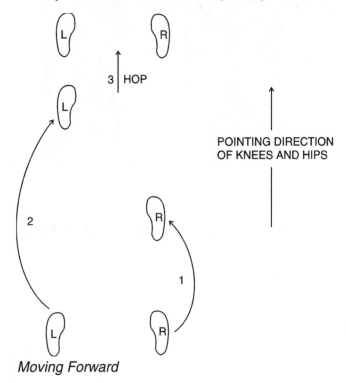

Moving Forward

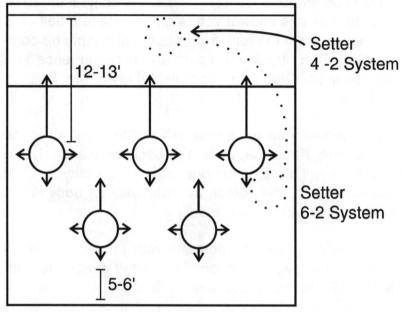

W Serve Reception Pattern (Five Players)

Communication

Don't be afraid to talk (yell, if that's what it takes) to let your teammates know if you're going to take a ball or to let them know if the ball is in or out. It shouldn't be complicated. Don't try to formulate an entire sentence in a split second. Keep it to one syllable. Mine. Me. Ball. In. Out.

Sometimes your teammate will yell for the ball at the same time. If that happens, the backrow player should make the call. If both the front and backrow player yell at the same time, the person who gets his/her body in position first should take the ball.

As you get more comfortable with movement, you'll learn how to avoid collisions by moving parallel to your teammate but not in the same lateral path.

Gym/Home Drills

1. **Lateral Drills:** Do the step-hop between two cones that are eight to 10 feet apart.

2. **Straight Line Drills:** Set up six to 10 portable cones in a straight line. Run forward or move laterally by doing the step-hop around the cones. Think about quick foot movement, and step as close as possible to the base of the cone.

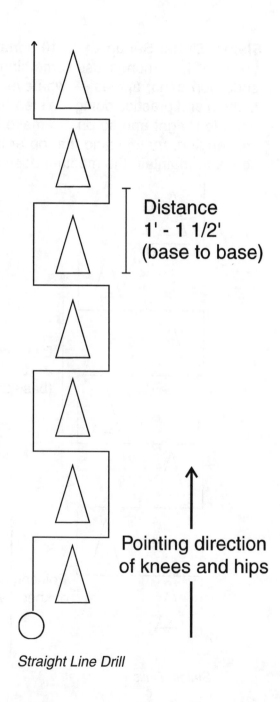

Distance
1' - 1 1/2'
(base to base)

Pointing direction
of knees and hips

Straight Line Drill

3. Slalom Drills: Set up six to 10 portable cones (If you don't have cones, use something else: chairs, soda pop cans, apples — whatever) in a slalom fashion and practice doing the step-hop to the left, right, left, right and so on. To make it even more challenging, try touching the top or bottom of the cones to maintain the medium posture.

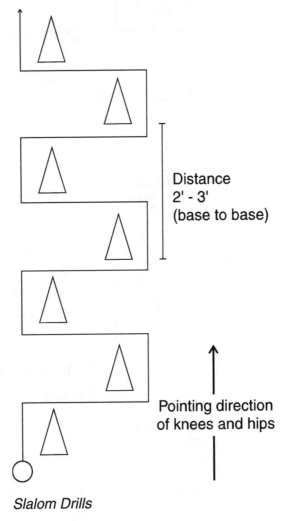

Distance
2' - 3'
(base to base)

Pointing direction
of knees and hips

Slalom Drills

4. Line Drills: Start at the end line and run to the 10-foot line. Touch the 10-foot line with one foot and return to the end line. Try it with all four types of movement: forward, backward and sideways to the left and right.

5. Box Drills: Use an area at least 10' x 10' but no bigger than 15' x 15'. Mark it off by using cones or lines. Move side to side, forward and backward within the box.

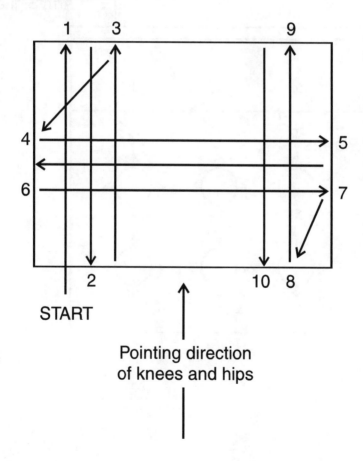

6. Four Direction: Players react to coach's arm signal, moving up, back or side-to-side.

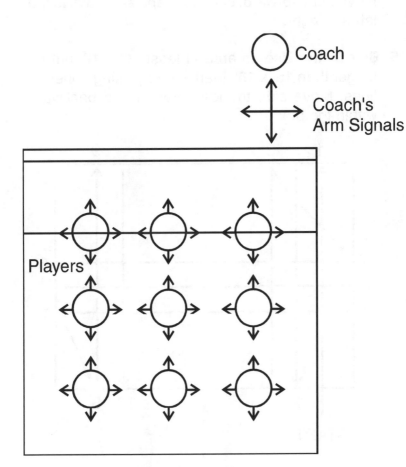

Elaine Youngs — USA Women's Team

II. Passing

Cue word: *Platform*
Key phrase: — Arms away from body
                  — Arms tilted to target

Cue word: *Track*
Key phrase: — Follow the ball from the server's
                  toss and contact to your arms

In the mid '70s, when I saw the world champion Polish men's team play in Chicago, I went up to the setter after the match and told him how great I thought he was. He smiled and said: "I run in; I put my hands up; there's a ball there; I set it."

That, in a nutshell, is the essence of passing. Great setters, no matter how talented, can't have a great match without support from their passers. If the passes are good, the whole offense clicks. But if they send the setters to the water cooler to make the set, the offense will surely break down.

Like defense in basketball, passing is a skill that gets lost among more glamorous pursuits. We all love to see Michael Jordan do those spinning, juking, double-pump jams. But do you ever see highlights of him playing defense on the evening sports wrap? No. Because defense isn't that exciting. Same thing with volleyball. The hitters get all the kudos, and hitting is the way you get noticed by the fans and become a star. But passing, like defense in basketball, is the path to being a complete player and helping your team win. And that makes it one of the most if not the most important skill in the sport. Hitters are a dime a dozen. But if you're a good passer, it will set you apart and your coach will find a spot for you on the court. Guaranteed.

The Ready Position/Tracking

The server on the other side of the net is at the end-line, ready to put the ball in play. What should you be doing? Getting into your medium position. Remember, your feet should be shoulder-width apart, one foot should be slightly ahead of the other and your heels should be off the floor with the weight distributed on the inside of the feet. Keep your knees bent. Focus on the ball as soon as the server tosses it and track it throughout the toss, the server's contact, its flight and your contact.

The *Platform*

The biggest key to becoming a great passer is learning how to form a ***platform***. A ***platform*** gives you a flat surface that you can point in the direction of the setter and use to make a good pass. It should never bend. Think of what a volleyball does when you bounce it off a bumpy surface. The first time, it might ricochet to the left. The second time to the right. If the surface isn't flat, it could bounce anywhere. But if it's flat, like a board, the ball will bounce the same way on the first pass as it does on the 43rd. And that's the key to consistent passing. A good, true rebound. Every time.

To create a perfect **platform**, join your hands together so your thumbs are parallel and facing away from your body. Lock your elbows as close together as you can. Imagine that your arms are tied together with a rope, and move them in unison. Shrug your shoulders. That helps relax your arms and elongates them to form a better platform. Make sure that your arms are away from your body. This will give you more control and a more fluid contact instead of a herky-jerky motion.

Moving to the Ball

It would be nice if the serve always came right to you, but, of course, it won't. Good passers learn how to adjust to serves that are in front of them or to their right or left. The key is to make your move without ruining your platform. To do that, you need to drop the lead shoulder and extend your platform to one side or the other. If the ball is breaking to your right, step to your right and drop your left shoulder. If it's breaking left, step left and drop your right shoulder. If it's in front of you or behind you, step forward or backward and drop one shoulder depending on which way the ball is breaking.

If you're able to do this with every serve it will allow you to keep your platform pointing to the target (the setter). Pretend there's an imaginary arrow coming out of the board. The arrow should be pointing to the setter, not toward the ceiling or the bottom of the net. Tilt your arms to target. If you're able to point it toward the setter every time, your passes will be consistently good.

Two common mistakes inexperienced players make are not getting to the ball and swiveling their arms to reach a tough serve instead of dropping their shoulder. When you make those mistakes, your arms will face toward the ceiling and the ball will glance off them and go behind you. That takes the setter out of the offense and means one of your teammates is going to have to scramble and make a great bump set from deep in the court for your team to even get a swing at the ball. Remember, when the ball is above your waist and to your side, drop the shoulder and keep the platform pointing to target so your pass goes forward to the setter (see p. 21).

Drop the lead shoulder

Contact

The ball should be contacted between the elbow and the wrist, preferably closer to the wrist. If the serve is right to you, your arms should be at about waist or belly button level when the ball strikes them. Remember to make sure your arms are away from your body when the ball makes contact. If they are too close, it's hard to control the pass because you won't have a good platform or angle to your target. If you have to shift to the left or right, the contact point will be chest level. But it shouldn't ever be higher than chest level because that eliminates the platform.

Always tilt your ***platform*** toward the target. Players often make the mistake of pointing their platform toward the ceiling as opposed to tilting it toward the setter. This makes it difficult to be accurate.

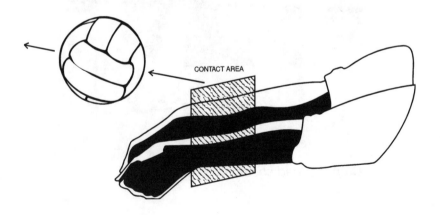

CONTACT AREA

Tilting the passing platform

Vision

One thing that makes a player a great passer is excellent vision. (That includes depth perception, peripheral vision and *tracking* the path of the ball.)

It's a good idea to get your eyes examined in case you need corrective lenses. Good sight is essential to developing excellent court vision.

Gym Drills

1. **Four-way passes:** Have someone toss you the ball so you have to move in, move back and move to your right and left. This forces you to adjust to the ball by dropping your shoulder and keeping your platform pointing to target.
2. **Live Serves:** Mark off six Xs on the court and have someone serve to you at each one so you can develop the versatility to pass from anywhere on the court.
3. **Ten-foot Line:** Stand on the 10-foot line and have someone hit ball after ball to you at normal serve velocity.

Home Drills

1. Pass to yourself. Let the ball travel about five feet above your head. This is good for developing your platform and improving ball control.
2. Once you've become good at Drill No. 1, it's important to begin passing to a horizontal target. Use a sturdy wall or a flat section of your garage door and draw a target. Pass to yourself over and over, thinking about maintaining a flat platform and pointing your platform to the target.

Lori Endicott — USA Women's Team

III. Setting

Cue word: *Face*
Key phrase: — Knees, hips, shoulders to target

Cue word: *Forehead*
Key phrase: — Ball set from forehead

Setting is probably the most underdeveloped skill in American volleyball, and there's a simple reason for that. Up until 1965, Americans were taught to receive overhand rather than with the bump. The great players of the '50s and early '60s passed every ball with their hands, and, by using their hands throughout a match, they developed solid setting skills.

Nowadays, because everybody uses the bump forearm pass, setting has settled somewhere between a specialized skill and a lost art. Finding players who do it really well isn't a whole lot easier than finding a bargain at the airport gift shop. Which means that there's room for good setters on teams of all levels: high school, club, college. Even international.

Mastering the fundamentals is the key to becoming a good setter. That may sound obvious, but you'd be surprised at the number of players who skip the basics and try to be fancy right away. Being fancy should be low on your priority list. First, you want to be good. Then you want to be smart. And finally, if you've mastered both, you can try fancy.

Get there on time/Face target

Young setters often get to their position at the net about the same time as the pass. That's a bad habit. If you don't get there before the ball does, you're going to be in an awkward position and you'll probably get called for a lot of throws. Your goal should be to get there as quickly as possible and to *face* the target, getting hips, knees and shoulders pointing in the direction you will be setting.

As soon as the serve is hit, sprint to a zone a little to the right of the net's center (see p. 29). Ideally, you want to be there before the passer touches the ball. Be aggressive and think about attacking the ball. It's a lot like being a shortstop in baseball or softball. You don't want a grounder to eat you up while you stand and wait for it, you want to take control of the situation by charging in and grabbing it. If the ball is moving slowly, don't relax. Your objective should be to go full speed on every play and get to the net. That way your teammates will know they can rely on you.

A good way to shorten the time it takes to get to the net is to measure the number of steps and determine the shortest route. After you've done that, practice the steps so they become second nature and you don't have to think about them during a match. Taking one or two fewer

The setting zone is to the right of center

Forehead/hand contact — front and side views

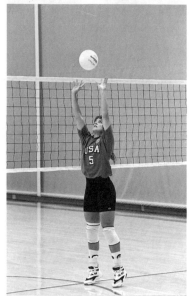

Follow through — front and side views

steps can make a big difference in getting to your position on time.

When you're on defense and digging, you have to determine if the ball is going to be hit at you before you run to the net.

Forehead/Hand contact

Always set the ball right on your *forehead*, just above your eyes. Get your midline behind the ball. As it comes into your hands, catch it for a split second, bring it in to your *forehead* and then release it in the direction that your knees, hips and shoulders are facing (see p. 30). The position of your hand on the ball is important in making a clean set. Don't use your finger tips or palms. Use the pads of your second and third fingers and thumbs. The fourth finger and pinky should only be used to brace the ball.

Release

If you look at slow motion video, you'll notice that great setters actually catch the ball and then release it with a quick throw. People always talk about soft hands. Well, soft hands are really just hands that can catch the ball quickly, bring it down so it almost touches the *forehead* and then throw it before anybody can tell.

Don't push your luck. If you're holding onto the ball for more than a split second, the ref will call it.

Make sure your fingers are flexible and not stiff and flat. That way the ball will come out clean and won't spin or go in a direction you don't want it to go. Extend your arms fully on the follow-through (see p. 30).

Bend your knees

Bending your knees at about a 45-degree angle will give you the strength to push the ball far enough for outside sets. At the international level, setters don't bend their knees a lot because they have to disguise the direction of their sets and bending makes it easier for the defense to determine where the ball is going. The setters on Asian teams are particularly good at using their wrists, not their legs. That makes them tough to read.

But remember, good should come before fancy. Unless you're starting for the national team, you shouldn't be worried about disguising your sets. To be a solid, dependable setter you need to be accurate, and bending your knees will improve your accuracy.

Backsetting

Aim your hands toward the ceiling, and point your fingers back at the target. After releasing the ball, arch your back slightly.

The correct back arch and hand/finger position for backsetting

Backsetting sequence

The all-around game

Having good technique is only part of becoming a great setter. Ideally, a setter should be able to block, play defense and set. But that's unusual, even at the international level.

At the international level, U.S. setter Lori Endicott is an average defensive player, but she makes up for it by being a great blocker. You have to at least be able to do one of the two. If you're a weak blocker, work on your defensive skills. If you're a weak defensive player, work on your blocking. If you're not good at either, you'll be a liability on the court even if you're a good setter.

Emergency setting

Don't ignore the bump set. You won't always get good passes. When you can't get your forehead behind the ball, switch to the bump set.

The key to a good bump set is getting under the ball, pointing to target, exaggerating the use of your legs and stopping your follow-through when it gets to the level of your chest.

Just like in passing, drop the shoulder that's closest to target if you're sideways. Move your arms and legs up toward the ball in a simultaneous motion.

Leadership

The other big thing a setter should have is the ability to communicate with teammates. Setters are often referred to as "Quarterbacks" or "Point Guards" because they run the offense. If you're going to be effective, you need to be a bit of a psychologist who can take guff from teammates with a smile and push the right buttons to get them performing at their peak level.

Some players need to be encouraged with compliments, others need to be kicked in the butt. It's your job as the setter to determine who needs what and dish it out when it's appropriate.

Drills

1. Set the ball to yourself two to three feet above your forehead — try this both standing and sitting.

2. Set the ball off a wall one foot away. Keep your forehead facing the wall.

3. Set the ball to yourself four to six feet above your head.

4. Set off the wall standing six to eight feet away. Draw a line on the wall at eight feet and set to that height.

Tara Cross-Battle — USA Women's Team

IV. Hitting

Cue word: *Wait*
Key phrase: — Before taking a step, wait to
         identify height, speed and location
         of the set.

Cue word: *Accelerate*
Key phrase: — Build speed, increase momentum
         of each step in your approach.
         — Once you start, don't slow down.

Cue word: *Reach*
Key phrase: — Contact the ball high and in front
         of you.
         — Extend your hitting arm.

You walk into an empty gym with a few friends and see half a dozen volleyballs lying around, what's the first thing you're going to do? Practice passing? Yeah, sure. Setting? Nope. Chances are, if you're like 99 percent of the population, you'll hit.

It's like basketball. The first thing you learn to do is shoot because shooting is a lot of fun. Nobody grabs a ball during half-time of an NBA championship game and goes outside to work on their bounce pass.

This is why, even though spiking is the most complicated bio-mechanical skill in volleyball, I don't worry too
much about players learning it because it's the first thing
they want to learn. But to do it right, there are some important steps to follow.

In this chapter, I've broken it down into three parts:

1. The Approach
2. The Take-off
3. The Contact

Once you've mastered these three, you'll have the solid
base you need to be a consistent hitter. Then you'll be
able to add to your repertoire and drive your opponents
crazy with a wide variety of effective shots.

The descriptions below will refer to a regular high outside set to the left front hitter.

The Approach

I like the three-step (step-close) approach. For right
handers, the first step is a short running step with the
left foot. Begin this first step a fraction of a second before the ball is at the peak of its arc (halfway in its flight)
from the setter's hands. *Wait*.

The second step is a braking step which lands on the
heel of the right foot. Your arms should extend all the
way back before you plant your foot.

The third step is a closing step, which lands on the ball (toe) of the foot. During this step the arms drive down and help get the body off the floor.

Remember, you must **accelerate** throughout the three-step sequence.

As the arms drive down and then up, you are at the take-off point. The approach pattern should be 45 degrees to the net, starting a little off the court about 12 feet from the net (see p. 46).

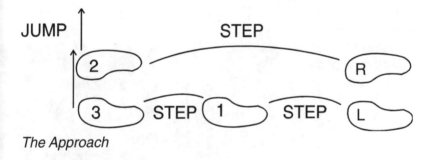

The Approach

Front view approach sequence

Note:
- *Arm movements (photos 1-8).*
- *Left leg plant (side of left foot parallel to center line and net) (photo 7).*
- *Bow and arrow of hitting arm and left arm pointing toward ball (not in photo) (photo 8).*
- *Position of ball in relation to hitter (in front) (photo 8).*
- *Eye and head position (photo 8).*
- *Back arch of the hitter (photo 8).*

1.

2.

6.

7.

3.   4.   5.

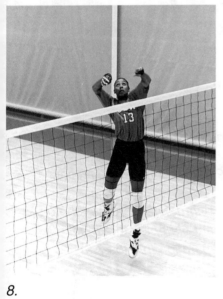

8.

9.

1.   2.

5.   6.   7.

Side view approach sequence

Note:
- The player starts 12 ft. from the net and to the left of the sideline (photo 1).
- Her approach will take her 8-9 ft. in a horizontal direction before she jumps.
- Her long step and the backward thrust of her arms (photo 5).
- The arm drive down and the plant of her left foot (photo 6).
- Her take-off and arm swing preparation (photos 7-9).

3.   *4.*

8.   *9.*

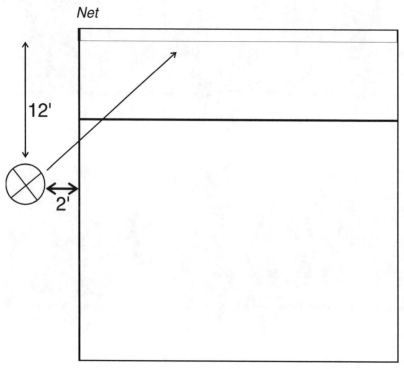

Starting Position and Approach Angle

⊗ = *Starting position on regular high set to left front hitter*

↗ = *Approach angle*

The Take-off

Plant both feet a shoulder width apart. Bend your knees at a 80 to 100 degree angle and extend your arms all the way behind you. (See p. 48). As you're about to jump (before your last closing step), pull your arms forcefully downward, then upward. This motion, when coordinated with your leg extension and eventual take-off, can increase your jump by several inches.

As you become airborne, your hitting arm should be cocked back in a bow-and-arrow position (see photo) and your non-hitting arm should be pointing at the ball.

The take-off spot should put you in the air a full arm's length behind the ball after you've jumped and your momentum has carried you forward a bit.

Take-off sequence

1.   2.

Note:

- *The knee bend and foot plant (photo 1).*
- *The arm drive (photos 1 & 2).*
- *The arm movement and bow-and-arrow positon (photos 3 & 4).*
- *For a quick set, there may not be time to point at the ball with the non-hitting arm.*

3.

4.

The Contact

Reach, extend your arm fully and strike the ball with the heel, palm and fingers of your hand. Ideally, the ball should be 1/2 to one foot in front of your head when you make contact.

Inexperienced players often make the mistake of contacting the ball behind or directly above their heads. That causes two problems. One, it takes away their vision of the court, preventing them from seeing the block and defense. Two, it slows down the speed of the spike.

For better control, spread your fingers while keeping your hand and wrist firm. If you're tall and/or jump well and can get above the net, make contact at the top of the ball. If you're short and/or do not jump well or you're far away from the net, strike underneath the ball to create maximum topspin.

Okay, now that we've covered the basics, let's talk about variety. First off, I think the most important thing to do is learn how to hit hard before you try mixing in tips or any other fancy shot. Start by learning the hard cross-court (angle) spike, then work on the line shot. After that, you can throw in the wipe, roll and tip.

*Contact and reach on a
high outside set*

*Contact and reach on a quick
set*

Cross-court (Angle)

One of the big keys to an angle hit is positioning your shoulders behind the ball. Point your knees and hips to the cross-court sideline on your opponent's side. To get a sharp angle, you must turn your wrist toward the sideline and then snap it down on the ball.

The Line

Start off the same way you did on the cross-court spike. Turn your body as you prepare to hit, but don't over rotate your shoulders. They should be parallel to the net after contact.

Make contact straight through the ball. Guide it by rotating your upper body. When you get more advanced, try just turning your wrist. That makes it tougher for the blockers because it isn't easy to read.

Remember: Don't be too fine when hitting the line. It may be a bad rhyme, but it's a great tip. Too often players think the best way to make a good line hit is to place the ball an inch or two inside the line. But when you try to be that perfect, you're going to hit more balls out than in. And that isn't the way to help your team win a match.

If you're a right-hander and you're hitting on the left, never let the ball cross your face before you contact it. On the right side, hit the ball just as it passes your face. Do the opposite if you're left-handed — on the left let the set cross your face and go to your left shoulder before you swing. On the right, hit the ball when it's in front of your left shoulder.

After you've established a hard hit down the line and cross-court (angle), you need to develop a roll shot, a wipe shot and a tip.

The Roll

Use the same approach you would if you were going to swing away. Then, at the last second, make contact underneath or behind the ball and roll your hand over it. Don't hit this shot too low or it will go right into the blockers.

1.   2.

The roll shot — note how the hand rolls and the wrist snaps in photo 2

For a roll shot, contact should be in back of or under the ball

The Wipe

During a game you'll often have to face a two-player block. If you can attack around the blockers, go for it. But there will be times when the block looks like The Great Wall of China. This is when it's critical to have a shot that is played off the blockers.

1. **The Hard Wipe** — Aim at the line and turn your wrist to flick the ball off the arms or hands of the end (line) blocker. Be patient. If you rush your shot you may throw it out of bounds without touching the blocker (see p. 57).

2. **The Soft Wipe** — When you're truly trapped by a penetrating block, hit the ball softly into it so it will deflect back onto your side of the net and be playable.

Remember, if you hit a hard, low shot into a block it will result in a straight-down stuff block for your opponent.

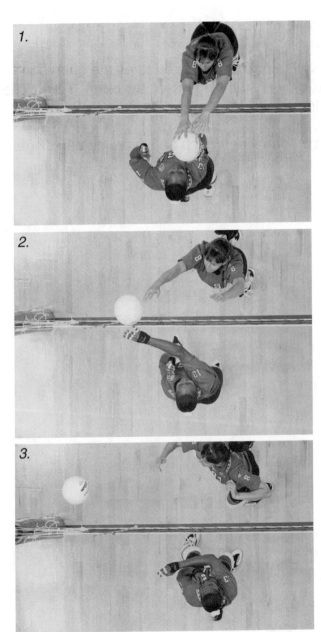

*Tara Cross-Battle hits the hard wipe shot off
Tammy Liley's block*

The Tip

This is sometimes referred to as the open hand dink. It is struck with the fingers of an open hand. The wrist should be stiff.

Use a normal approach and make sure to disguise your shot until the last second (see p. 59).

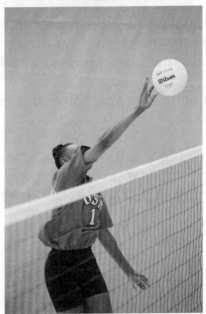

Excellent tip shot form

Home Drills:

1. A good way to practice hitting when you're first starting out is to stand on the floor and do repetitions without jumping. Beginning players shouldn't jump. It's essential to master the hitting motion before you complicate it with the jump. Work on extending your arm, striking the ball a little bit to the right of your nose (left if you're left handed) and six inches in front of your face.

2. If you're by yourself, hit the ball with a bounce on the floor or hit it against a garage or wall. Stand a little closer to the wall than you do when you're practicing your serve.

3. Get a piece of netting, tie it around the ball, hang the ball in the netting up on a tree branch and practice approaching, jumping and hitting.

4. Have someone toss you some sets. ***Wait, accelerate, reach.***

5. When you've got a friend to practice with, have him or her throw you the ball, pass it back, approach on your friend's set and take a swing.

Hitting Summary
The quick set approach take-off and contact sequence.

1. Watch the pass to the setter   2. First step

3. Beginning of second step

4. Arm drive and end of second long braking step

5. Foot plant and finish of arm drive

6. Take-off

7. Hitting arm back —
shoulders are open to the
setter and left shoulder is
perpendicular to the net

8. Arm swing

9. Contact

Karch Kiraly — Former USA Men's Team Player

V. Blocking

Cue word:	*Front*
Key phrase:	— Position body in front of hitter's striking arm
Cue word:	*Penetrate*
Key phrase:	— Go directly over net
	— Press (extend) with arms and shoulders
Cue word:	*Hands*
Key phrase:	— Block ball with your hands
	— Spread your fingers

Chances are, you don't jump like Karch Kiraly or Teee Williams. If you do, send me a postcard. But if you don't, don't worry. It isn't a big deal. Players get by just fine by knowing a few secrets, and you can do the same.

Many people think great blockers have to be giants who tower over the net. That isn't true, even though most international women's players can jump high enough to reach over 10 feet, and the men can jump and reach over 11. But no matter how high you reach, what's more important is *penetrating* and going directly over the net.

The real key is to be a smart blocker with good technique. If you can read the opposing team's offense, time your jump and **penetrate** over the net, you'll be a good blocker even if you're not a giant or a jumping monster.

And keep in mind, it doesn't take as much time to become a good blocker as it does to become a good defensive player. Also, how many balls are you going to dig straight on? Against good hitters, not many. But if you're a good blocker, you'll make your team's defense a lot better.

Reading

The first thing you have to do as a blocker is watch the opponent to see what's happening on the other side of the net. If an opposing player has just made a pass or a dig, following the flight of the ball can help you determine where you should set up your block. For instance, a setter can only set the middle on a perfect pass. If the ball is shanked, then it's probably going to be a high outside set. The same is true if the ball is dug in the backcourt because the setter will have to rush to get there or another player will have to make the set. Either way, the set will probably be high and outside.

Until you get to the college level, your main concern will almost always be to block the big hitter on the other team. If you take out the best player, you'll put your team in a good position to win. So put yourself in the optimum position to block their best player.

Footwork

Once you've decided where you should be on the net, you have to get directly in front of the hitter's arm as quickly as possible. To move side to side most efficiently, use shuffle steps. Advanced players use cross-over steps. Use them if you're comfortable.

A good way to check yourself to make sure you're doing the side steps correctly is to pretend there's a line drawn between your right and left toes. If it's parallel to the center line, you're doing it right. If it isn't, try again.

Shuffle step *(Motion shown left to right)*

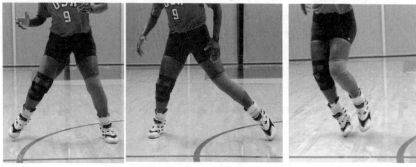

Note that the feet never cross over in the shuffle step.

Cross-over step *(Motion shown right to left)*

The arm motion of the cross-over step is similar to a spiking

approach. This is a dynamic, aggressive technique.

Watch the hitter

Once you've followed the path of the ball from the passer (or digger) to the setter, watch the set direction and then shift your attention to the hitter. A big mistake many inexperienced players make is watching the ball as the hitter attacks it. That doesn't do you much good. You should watch the hitter, noticing the approach, the jump, the shoulder positioning and the arm swing. If you do that, you'll have a better chance of figuring out where the ball and the hitter will intersect. Then you can position yourself to block the ball.

Front the hitter

Get your body positioned immediately in *front* of the hitter's striking arm.

Fronting the hitter

Wait

How many times have you seen a blocker jump and then fall before the ball is hit? It happens all the time. A lot of players think that you're supposed to jump at the same time as the attacker, but think about it. It takes time for the ball to go from the hitter's hand to your side of the net. You'll be on your way down to the floor if you jump simultaneously with the hitter. By jumping a split second after the hitter, you reach your peak height at the right time.

Jump

Usually, you coil and bend about 45 degrees before making your jump. But do whatever feels most comfortable. Remember, the important thing is to keep your chest parallel to the net.

One good way to increase height is to use your arms to propel yourself into the air. Be careful not to hit the net on your way up. The best way to do this is to turn sideways with your left shoulder perpendicular to the net. Use a three-step spiking approach, and then swing your arms to help you gather more momentum in your jump (see pp. 68-69).

The blocking jump

Penetrate

I think ***penetrating*** over the net is the most important aspect of blocking. Too often players put their arms straight up when they block giving the attacker more room to hit.

What you should do is reach as far over the net as you can to take up your opponent's air space. Even if you only ***penetrate*** over the net an inch farther than you would if you were blocking straight up and down, that covers a much larger area in the back court and gives your defense a better chance to pick up the ball.

Penetrating over the net

Elaina Oden penetrates, spreading her fingers apart

Hands

Always attempt to block the ball with your **hands**, not your forearms. As you block the ball, your palms should face the floor.

Your **hand** position is different depending on which side of the court you're on. If you're the right side blocker, you should have your right hand tilted toward the cross-court. If you're on the left, point cross-court with your left hand. This will help prevent you from getting tooled by the hitter.

If you're the right front, you want to have your left hand on the ball when you block line. If you're giving up the line, your right hand should be on the ball. Do just the opposite if you're the left front end blocker. Make sure your fingers are spread as you're **penetrating** and blocking (see pp. 75 and 77).

In the middle

If you're the middle blocker, your job is to close to the end blockers, seal the seam and take the angle shot. To put up a formidable two-person block, you have to close all the way to your end blocker. Leaving even the slightest gap opens the seam (the area between the middle and the end blocker) for the hitter. If you're moving to your right and you're the middle blocker, your right arm should almost touch the left arm of your end blocker.

The middle blocker (No. 8) has closed the block by moving to her left next to the left front outside blocker. Note how the two players' arms leave no seam between the blockers.

Home Drills

1. Hang a rope or a clothes line at net height in the backyard and practice jumping over and over with your arms up in blocking position.

2. Practice shuffling and then jump and penetrate over the rope. Go to your right and left.

3. Do the same with the cross-over.

4. Have a friend stand on a chair and hit balls at you. Practice penetrating over the rope.

Gym Drills

1. Use the home drills with the net.

2. Have a teammate and/or coach stand on a chair three to four feet from the net and hit balls at you jumping on either side of the net. Work on penetration and blocking with your hands.

Caren Kemner — USA Women's Team

VI. Defense

Cue word: *Stop*
Key phrase: — Stop your feet at hitter's contact

Cue word: *Low*
Key phrase: — Contact the ball from a low body
                      position
                — Come up to meet the ball

Cue word: *Arms*
Key phrase: — Play ball with both arms as much as
                      possible

I learned to play volleyball on an asphalt court. Let me tell you, there's no better incentive than asphalt to develop your skills in reading the other team's offense and anticipating where the ball is going. If you rely on your ability to dive for shots on an unforgiving surface like asphalt, you don't have a whole lot of skin left at the end of the day.

Contrary to popular belief, there's a lot more to defense than diving, rolling and sprawling for the ball. These moves look spectacular, but they should only be made in emergency situations. I see a lot of kids working on them before they learn how to read a hitter's arm swing or a setter's set direction. Knowing where the ball is likely to go is a lot more valuable than being good at diving around like a maniac.

To be a great defensive player, you have to know what to do before the ball comes to your side of the net. Like I mentioned earlier, great players are able to achieve their level of play by using their brains as well as their athletic ability.

And the process starts long before the ball gets to you.

The Attitude

Before we go any further, I'd like to talk a little about the importance of having the right mind set. When you walk on the court, whether it's practice or a match, your goal should be to not let one ball hit the floor. That's the way you drive yourself to become a great defensive player. Just get there. No matter what.

Whenever the ball is in play, follow it with your eyes. Always be thinking that every ball is coming in your direction. That way, you'll always be ready to make the play.

And keep in mind, you're responsible for a defensive area, not just one precise spot on the court. (See diagram p. 83).

Starting Position

Get into a pre-determined stationary positioning. (This will depend on your coach's scheme for team defense.) When the ball crosses the net into your opponent's court, you should be in your medium position, prepared to react quickly and intersect the ball. In indoor volleyball, you position yourself around the block. That determines your area of responsibility.

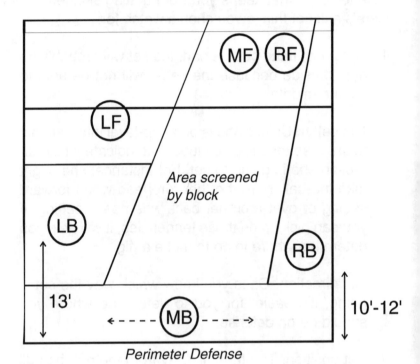

Perimeter Defense

- *Setter = RB*
- *RB has dinks on right side*
- *LF has dinks on left side*
- *MB stays on endline; he must also adjust to the seam in the block*

Reading

Reading is what keeps you from getting skinned knees. Here's a list of things you should watch for:

1. The pass. If the pass is bad, the set will probably go high outside because the setter will not be able to set the middle.

2. The setter. Unless she is on a top-level international team, a setter will give clues that indicate which direction she is going to set. For instance, she might take the ball in front of her forehead when forward setting or over-arch her back when back setting. If you can pick up on these tendencies, it will help you determine where to go to make a dig.

3. Set direction. Once you know which way the set is going, it's easier for you to determine where you should be on defense.

4. Set position. The further away from the net the ball is, the flatter and closer it will be to the top of the net when it goes over and the longer it will take to get to the defender. If the ball is on top of the net, the blocker has to defend it or it will probably be hit straight down to the floor.

5. Attacker approach. Two things to watch for here: Is the hitter coming at an angle or straight at the net? Is the hitter on time or late? If the hitter is coming in at an angle, he will probably hit cross court. But when hitters approach the net straight on, they'll often hit

the ball down the line. An attacker who is late getting to a set will probably just try to get the ball in. If you're blocking a late-arriving attacker, wait before you jump.

6. Look for hitter tendencies. Only the world's very best attackers have such a good variety of shots that they can hit anything at any time. Most hitters have a favorite shot. Some players might like to hit line and extreme cross-court angles while others may prefer hitting between the two blockers.

Making the Dig

Once you get to the spot where you're going to dig the ball, make sure you *stop* your feet. They should be a little more than shoulder width apart and you should be crouched down *low* to the floor. Get in a comfortable position. Your back should be hunched but not too hunched. Stay on the balls of your feet. A common mistake a lot of players make is standing on their heels or not staying *low* enough to the ground. If you're on your heels or up too high, chances are you won't be able to dig a ball that's hit right at you. A big part of being a good digger is having a balanced, stable body position that allows you to move forward.

When the ball arrives, don't swing your *arms*. Come up and meet it. The key is to have a stable platform and absorb the impact of the ball when it hits. We'll call it cushioning the dig. If your *arms* are too rigid, the ball may pop over the net or out of bounds. But if you give an inch or two on impact, you'll have a much better chance of popping it straight up where your teammate can get it. Be sure to keep your arms tight together, though. If they're loose, they may come apart when the ball hits. Play the ball with two *arms*.

Note the low position of both players.

Footwork

You should always put your right foot forward on the right side of the court and your left foot forward on the left. That way, you'll dig the ball into the court rather than sending it into the third row or over the net. Your objective is to dig the ball to the setter. Having the correct foot forward and facing your body and shoulders into the court will make it a lot easier.

Emergency Digs

Since you won't always be in a situation where you can make the perfect dig, it's essential for you to know how to adjust. Don't take that as an excuse to be lazy. Your first goal should be to get into your ideal position. But when you don't have time, try one of the following emergency digs:

1. Overhand — If the ball is up high, and you can't dig it with your regular platform, you have two options: the tomahawk and the one-hand knuckler. First, the tomahawk. Put both hands together and form a flat surface with your fists. Second, the one-hand knuckler. Bend your knuckles and pop the ball up with an open fist.

The tomahawk

The one-handed knuckler

2. The dive — Play the ball as you dive and follow-through by sliding on the court. Use both hands to push yourself back up.

3. The roll — Reach one arm out, play the ball and then roll over your shoulder in the direction you're moving.

The roll

4. The sprawl — Collapse forward to play the ball. Slide
   on the floor to get under it.

The sprawl

5. The spring-out — Thrust your body low to the floor, take one step or just "spring out" from a standing position. This is similar to the dive, but you are lower and closer to the floor.

The spring-out

Home Drills

1. Stand about eight or 10 feet away from a wall. Throw a ball off the wall and dig the rebound. It isn't easy to approximate a spiking angle, but just try to force yourself to get down low to play the ball.

2. Same drill as No. 1, except this time you have someone stand behind you and throw the ball off the wall so you can't see where it's going until it hits the wall.

3. Find a friend and have him stand on a chair and hit balls at you.

Gym Drills

1. Practice the dive, roll, sprawl and spring-out. Get up immediately.

Kristin Klein — USA Women's Team

VII. Serving

Cue word:	*Toss*
Key phrase:	— Toss ball in front of hitting shoulder

Cue word:	*Float*
Key phrase:	— Solid contact in center of ball, no spin

The way I look at it, serving is the only skill in volleyball that doesn't provide you with an excuse for screwing up. Think about it. If you make a bad pass it might be because you had to receive a great serve. A bad hit could be the result of a bad set. Nearly every skill involves some form of error correction. The setter corrects an inaccurate pass, the hitter corrects an inaccurate set and so on.

But serving is different. The success of a serve depends on you and you alone. If you hit your *floater* into the third row and send somebody's popcorn flying, you have no one to blame but yourself. Mastering a good serve is a simple matter of practicing until you're comfortable with it. It isn't always easy to work on the other skills by yourself, but all you have to do to polish your serve is get a ball and go to it.

Serving is a valuable scoring tool. Every time you go back to the end-line to put the ball in play, you have an opportunity to score a point without any help from your teammates. Your team might be down 14-12 in the fifth, and you could turn defeat into victory in less than a minute by striking four great serves in a row. That doesn't happen often, but it is possible.

In order of importance...

1. The first thing you need to learn is how to get the ball over the net and into the court. Putting it in play automatically forces your opponent to execute the side-out offense. If you're always hitting the ball into the net or out of bounds, it gives the other team a free side-out.

2. Develop a *floater*. That's the first serve you should learn. A *floater* is easier than a standing top spin serve or a jump serve, and it's often extremely effective because it wavers back and forth like a drunk mosquito and is difficult to pass.

3. Work on your accuracy. Look for the weak passer. If you have a choice between serving to Karch Kiraly or Homer Simpson, pick Homer. There's no sense making it easier on the other team by serving to their strongest passer.

4. Refine your *floater* so you can serve it with a low trajectory. The closer the serve is to the net, the tougher it is to pass. A perfect serve clears the net

by about two inches, but it's pretty tough to do that on a regular basis. If you can consistently serve about a foot over the net you'll have a lot of success.

5. Put a little steam on the *floater*. Sending it over the net with good velocity forces the opponent to react quicker. And when they have less time to make a decision, there's more of a chance for an error.

6. Work on a topspin serve. This is fairly rare, but it shouldn't be because it's a good weapon. It's easier to serve than a jump serve and it can be almost as effective.

7. The jump serve. There's a good reason this is last on the list. It's an advanced skill, and you shouldn't bother with it until you've mastered all the others. As volleyball has evolved over the last 10 years, the jump serve has become a big factor in the international game. If you're a good jump server, you'll score a lot of points for your team.

The Floater

I'll start off with the ***toss*** because I think it's extremely important. I played a lot of tennis when I was a kid, and coaches always told me the toss was 75 percent of a tennis serve. That's about right for volleyball, too. If your toss is all over the place, you'll never be a consistent server.

The ***toss*** for the floater should be in front of the hitting shoulder, just above and a little bit to the right of your head. (For a left-handed player, it should be to the left of the head.) Hold the ball in the your fingers and upper palm, not in the middle of the palm. Don't put spin on the toss.

If, like many young players, you take a step when you serve, be sure to ***toss*** the ball further in front of you so you're not hitting it over your head. The ball should always be in front on the ***floater***.

A good way to test the location of your ***toss*** is to put a sheet of paper a couple of feet in front of you, ***toss*** the ball and see if it lands on the paper. If it does, you've got it right. If it lands on your head, keep practicing.

The big key to the ***floater*** is striking the ball in the center so it doesn't have any spin (see p. 102). That causes it to move up and down in the air and makes it tough for the passer to track. Draw your hitting arm back in a bow-and-arrow motion, toss the ball and make contact with the heel of your hand, not your fingers. If the ball hits your fingers your serve is bound to have backspin and that is an easy serve for the opponent to pass. Be sure your wrist is firm. Don't bend or snap it.

Hit the ball on its way up or at its peak, not on its way down. Unlike spiking, your arm should be bent rather than fully extended.

The ball should travel in a straight line as if it's following a string tied between the top of the net and your forehead. The flight is a flat, low trajectory like a line drive in baseball.

You'll want to experiment to find the best spot to stand when you serve the floater. If you start at the end-line, you'll have more accuracy but you won't be able to hit the ball as hard and get as much zigzag on the ball. If you stand really deep, you can blast the ball and make it swerve all over the place. Problem is, it may swerve out. Practice from various points until you figure out what works for you.

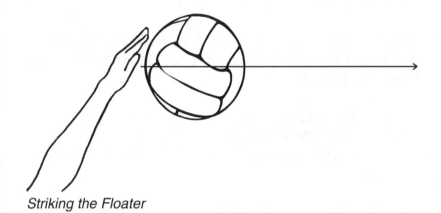

Striking the Floater

Contact of the floater serve

A back view of Yoko Zetterlund demonstrating the floater serve

Variations on the floater

There are several different ways to serve a floater: over-hand (as I described in the previous section), roundhouse or sidearm. The roundhouse serve is executed with a stiff arm while standing sideways to the net. It is used frequently by the Japanese and Chinese and is effective because it nose dives to the floor at about the time it clears the net. The roundhouse is contacted above the head or just in front of the head. Strike the center of the ball. Contact the sidearm above the waist and below the shoulder, standing sideways. This is a particularly effective serve for younger players.

The roundhouse floater

1.   2.

3.   4.   5.

Note:
- *The ball is hit sidearm, but through its center*
- *The ball is tossed in front and to the right of the server*
  (opposite for a left-hander)

Standing Topspin

This serve doesn't get used too often, but I like it because it has some of the same qualities as a jump serve but is easier to hit.

The toss for the standing topspin serve should be behind your head. If you toss in front of you like you would for the floater you'll probably hit the ball into the bottom of the net.

As the ball reaches its peak, arch your back, swing and strike the ball with the palm of your hand. As soon as you make contact, snap your wrist and use your abdominal muscles to whip your body and arm into the ball. This creates topspin like a jump serve.

The great thing about the topspin serve is it can be hit with a lot of velocity. Its flight path is more predictable than the floater, but if you can hit it hard enough you'll put your opponent on the defensive.

A standing topspin serve is a good change of pace to throw at the opponent after you've served several floaters in a row. It also works well against a team that doesn't move well or is intimidated by high-velocity serves.

The standing topspin serve

1.

2.

3.

4.

5.

Note:
- *The ball is tossed directly above the head (photo 4)*
- *The back is arched (photo 4)*
- *The arm snaps (photo 5)*

The Jump Serve

The jump serve toss needs to be way out in front of you because the momentum from your approach will carry you forward. Toss with one arm or two arms, whichever your prefer. The ball should go between four to six feet above your head.

Approach as if you are hitting a spike. As you can see from Teee Williams' demonstration in the photo sequence, the approach is similar to the spike approach except the player tosses to herself rather than awaiting the set. This means the timing for a jump serve is usually easier than the timing for a spike approach.

Remember, you can land on or in front of the endline as long as you contact the ball before you hit the floor.

The jump serve

1.

2.

3.

4.

5.

6.

7.

8.

Gym Drills

1. Stand at the endline and serve six balls in a row over the net.

2. Stand 10 to 15 feet away from the wall and serve 10 balls in a row. Remember, your objective is to make the ball *float* with no spin. Be sure to hit it in the center.

3. Put a line on the wall 7 1/2 feet above the floor. Stand 15 feet away and serve *floaters*. Try to hit the line as many times as you can.

4. Draw several target areas on the other side of the court and try hitting them.

Home Drills

1. Draw a line the height of the net on the garage and start serving from 15 feet. Move back to 20 feet, then 30. How many in a row can you get above the line?

Terry Liskevych — Coach, USA Women's Team

Conclusion

There are a number of elements to being a great player: jumping ability, quickness, hand-eye coordination, sport sense. But all of it is for naught unless you can truly take advantage of your potential. And the way you do that is by working hard.

All international players who have reached the top, from Karch Kiraly to Lori Endicott, have spent long hours enhancing their skills. If you follow their lead, you will also be able to maximize your talent and reach the peak of your game.

Lori Endicott and Bev Oden — USA Women's Team

Review of
Cue Words
and Key Phrases

General
Cue word: *Anticipate*
Key phrase: — Never be surprised
           — Expect every ball to
               come to you

Cue word: *Focus*
Key phrase: — Keep eyes on the ball
           — Maintain focus for entire
               play, rally, practice,
               game, match

Movement
Cue word: *Feet*
Key phrase: — Beat ball to spot
           — Stay on feet as much as
               possible

Cue word: — *Ready*
Key phrase: — Balanced to move in any
               direction

Passing
Cue word: *Platform*
Key phrase: — Arms away from body
           — Arms tilted to target

Cue word: *Track*
Key phrase: — Follow the ball from the
                     server's toss and
                     contact to your arms

Setting
Cue word: *Face*
Key phrase: — Knees, hips, shoulders
                     to target

Cue word: *Forehead*
Key phrase: — Ball set from forehead

Hitting
Cue word: *Wait*
Key phrase: — Before taking a step,
                     wait to identify height,
                     speed and location of
                     the set

Cue word: *Accelerate*
Key phrase: — Build speed, increase
                     momentum of each
                     step in your approach.
         — Once you start, don't
                     slow down

Cue word: *Reach*
Key phrase: — Contact the ball high
                     and in front of you
         — Extend your hitting arm

Blocking
Cue word: ***Front***
Key phrase: — Position body in front of hitter's striking arm

Cue word: ***Penetrate***
Key phrase: — Go directly over net
— Press (extend) with arms and shoulders

Cue word: ***Hands***
Key phrase: — Block ball with your hands.
— Spread your fingers

Defense
Cue word: ***Stop***
Key phrase: — Stop your feet at hitter's contact

Cue word: ***Low***
Key phrase: — Contact the ball from a low body position
— Come up to meet the ball

Cue word: ***Arms***
Key phrase: — Play ball with both arms as much as possible

<u>Serving</u>

Cue word: *Toss*
Key phrase: — Toss ball in front of
                   hitting shoulder

Cue word: *Float*
Key phrase: — Solid contact in center of
                   ball, no spin

About the Authors

In his 10 years as the head coach of the USA women's national volleyball team, Terry Liskevych has built the program from scratch following the 1984 Olympic Games and returned it to the forefront of the volleyball world. He directed the USA to its second ever Olympic medal (bronze) at the 1992 Olympics and the first gold medal at a major international tournament in the history of the women's program at the 1995 World Grand Prix. He will remain in his current position through the 1996 Olympic Games. He is the only coach to lead two USA volleyball teams into Olympic competition. Terry lives in Leucadia, California with his wife Nancy, son Mark and daughter Krista. Don Patterson is Executive Editor of Volleyball magazine and was previously a sports writer for the Los Angeles Times. He lives in Carlsbad, California with his wife Kendal and daughter Alex.